T0011345

WHAT IF YOU WERE ON THE AFRICAN FRONT IN WORLD WAR II?

AN INTERACTIVE HISTORY ADVENTURE

by Allison Lassieur

CAPSTONE PRESS
a capstone imprint

Published by You Choose, an imprint of Capstone
1710 Roe Crest Drive, North Mankato, Minnesota 56003
capstonepub.com

Library of Congress Cataloging-in-Publication Data is available on the Library of
Congress website.

ISBN 9781666390896 (hardcover)
ISBN 9781666390889 (paperback)
ISBN 9781666391046 (ebook PDF)

Summary: Takes readers through a series of choices placing them in the midst of
the action of World War II on the African front.

Editorial Credits
Editor: Mandy Robbins; Designer: Hilary Wacholz; Media Researcher: Jo Miller;
Production Specialist: Tori Abraham

Image Credits
Alamy: Classic Picture Library, 55, Everett Collection Historical, 98, FAY 2018,
39, FLHC 114A, 32, Niday Picture Library, 44, Nigel J Clarke, 62, Pictorial Press
Ltd, 86, RBM Vintage Images, 78, Roman Nerud, 89, Sueddeutsche Zeitung
Photo, 102, The Print Collector, 58, 67; Getty Images: Central Press / Stringer,
Cover (airplane), Haywood Magee, 18, Hulton Archive, 7, 81, Interim Archives, 11,
IWM, 72; Newscom: Official/Mirrorpix, 30; Shutterstock: Pyty, 106; Wikimedia:
NARA, 24, 75, National Museum of the U.S. Navy, Cover (explosion, tanks), 1

Design Elements
Shutterstock: Roman Amanov

TABLE OF CONTENTS

4

ABOUT YOUR ADVENTURE

YOU are fighting in North Africa during World War II (1939–1945). The hot desert sun beats down on you. You trudge through sand as tanks rumble across the desert. You're covered in grit that seems impossible to wash away.

Along the coast, the sounds of bombs and gunfire seem constant. Ships battle for control of the seas. Overhead, combat aircraft zoom through the clouds.

Turn the page.

When people think of World War II, desert battles don't often come to mind. But one of the most important World War II fronts was along the coast of Northern Africa. Many people fought and died there.

What will you do when you come face-to-face with the enemy? Will you stand your ground and fight? Do you have what it takes to survive? YOU CHOOSE which paths to take. Your choices will guide the story.

• Turn the page to begin your adventure.

CHAPTER 1

BATTLE IN THE SAND

When you volunteered to fight in World War II, you never imagined you'd be in the desert. The war began in Europe in 1939, when Adolf Hitler's Nazi Germany invaded Poland. In June 1940, Italy joined the war on Germany's side. Together, they made up part of the Axis powers. Its leaders wanted control of the Suez Canal in Egypt. The canal allowed supply ships through to Europe. British troops already protected the Suez Canal. Italian leader Benito Mussolini ordered Italian troops to attack them.

Hitler sent Nazi commander Major-General Erwin Rommel to help Italy win this part of North Africa. Rommel's nickname was the Desert Fox. His troops were known as the Afrika Korps.

British troops battled the Italians and the Afrika Korps along the North African coast. Neither side could defeat the other. The United States joined the war in 1941 on the side of Great Britain and the other Allied powers. In 1942, the U.S. sent troops to North Africa. They wanted to help the British defeat the Germans and the Italians and control the Mediterranean Sea.

The North African front is hot and deadly. But here you are. Are you ready to join the war on the North African front?

- To be a combat nurse, turn to page 10.
- To be an ace fighter pilot running secret missions and defending the troops, turn to page 42.
- To be a sailor on a massive warship battling enemy fleets and protecting supplies, turn to page 75.

CHAPTER 2

CARING FOR THE WOUNDED

In 1941, the United States joined World War II. You had just graduated from nursing school. The American armed forces needed medical personnel to care for soldiers. You volunteered as a nurse for the U.S. Army.

You were sent to a training camp in Louisiana. There, you learned how to use a gas mask and other army gear. You took classes on how to quickly care for patients in battle situations. You learned how to handle chemical and bomb attacks. Once training was over, you got your orders. Now you're going to the North African front.

There are several kinds of wartime hospitals. Field hospitals are near the front lines. Injured soldiers are brought directly there from the battlefield. Those who are badly wounded are moved to larger mobile evacuation hospitals. There, they'll get surgery or any other care they need. Then soldiers are either sent back to the front or on to a long-term recovery hospital.

U.S. Army nurses at a training center

Turn the page.

You board a ship for the long journey to Africa. Guard planes fly overhead to protect the ship from enemy attack. After many long days at sea, you arrive at the city of Oran on the North African coast. Your orders are to report to an evacuation hospital in a town somewhere in the desert. But before you land, you are given the option to work at a field hospital near the front line.

- To work at an evacuation hospital, go to page 13.
- To go to the field hospital near the front, turn to page 30.

Evacuation hospitals are farther from the fighting, which feels safer. A long line of large, open trucks sit at the dock. You squeeze into the back of one with some other nurses. For hours, the truck bumps along rough desert roads. The sun beats down, and sand seems to spit in your face.

Finally, you arrive in a small village surrounded by miles of desert. The largest building is an abandoned school. This will be your hospital. Inside, stacks of boxes and supplies sit everywhere. Everyone gets to work. You unpack crates of bandages, medicine, equipment, and other supplies. You organize the rooms into wards and set up operating rooms and labs. Soon, the wards are filled with tidy rows of army cots.

Turn the page.

It's not long before ambulance trucks filled with wounded soldiers appear. It's chaos as soldiers unload men on stretchers and doctors bark orders. Doctors and nurses must quickly decide who needs emergency attention and who can wait. Some nurses tend to patients with less threatening injuries.

- To help the doctors organize the wounded, go to page 15.
- To tend to less serious wounds, turn to page 21.

You step to the back of a truck of moaning, bleeding men. Medics unload stretchers of wounded. You stop each one, looking for an Emergency Medical Tag (EMT) pinned to his uniform. It's filled out with his name, his army unit, and his injury.

Most injured men have bullet wounds. Some have been hit by shrapnel. These bits of metal fly from exploding bombs or mines. Some soldiers have broken bones. A few can't be helped. Nothing in your training prepared you for this horror.

Doctors move quickly from stretcher to stretcher, assessing the wounds. They start preparing for surgery. Another nurse asks you for help with a soldier who collapsed. Just then, a doctor asks you to assist him in the operating room.

- To help the soldier, turn to page 16.
- To prep for surgery, turn to page 20.

He can't be more than 18 or 19 years old. He's got a bloody bandage wrapped around his leg. It looks broken. He wakes up and looks around, confused. You give him a few sips of water.

"What's your name, soldier?" you ask.

"Bobby," he mutters.

"You're going to be okay, Bobby."

A doctor removes the leg bandage and examines the break. Then he pulls you aside. Bobby will need surgery soon, but the break is not an emergency. Unfortunately, there are too many wounded here. It will be hours before the surgeons can get to him.

A medic tells you that an ambulance is taking nonemergency patients to a general hospital in Oran. But the bumpy roads could reinjure his leg.

- To send Bobby in the ambulance, go to page 17.
- To care for Bobby while he waits for surgery here, turn to page 18.

The doctor agrees that the risk of the ride is worth it. You take Bobby's hand and tell him, "You're going to go to a hospital in Oran. It's a few hours' ride from here. I'm going to give you something for your pain."

He looks frightened, and you squeeze his hand.

"These boys will take good care of you."

Two medics appear and lift Bobby's stretcher. The young soldier grabs your arm.

"Thank you," he whispers.

Then he disappears into the crowd of soldiers, doctors, nurses, and medics. As you watch him go, you know you'll never forget the first soldier you ever helped.

THE END

To follow another path, turn to page 9.
To learn more about the African front, turn to page 102.

You find one of the last empty cots and make Bobby comfortable. It's noisy and cramped. You bring Bobby water and take his temperature and blood pressure. You give him pain medicine and then check on a few other patients. It's dark by the time the medics come to get Bobby for surgery. By then, the wound is angry red. Infection has set in.

Nurses inspect a wounded soldier's leg.

A couple of hours later, the doctor finds you. He looks exhausted.

"I couldn't save the leg," he says. "The infection went too deep."

"Did we wait too long?" you ask, fearful of the answer.

The doctor shook his head. "I don't know if transporting him would have made any difference," was his weary reply. "We did the best we could."

It wasn't the outcome you'd hoped for, but at least Bobby is alive. So many soldiers aren't.

THE END

To follow another path, turn to page 9.

To learn more about the African front, turn to page 102.

The operating room buzzes with activity. White sheets hang from the ceiling to separate operating areas. Bare light bulbs dangle overhead. There's no time to think, as the first patient is dropped onto the table, moaning in pain. As soon as one surgery is over, medics whisk the patient away and put another one down. The floor is slick with blood. The terrible sights of gunshot wounds, missing limbs, and broken bones will never leave your mind.

By the end of your 12-hour shift, you know this isn't for you. The next day, you ask for a transfer to a hospital in Oran where nurses help injured soldiers recover. You'll still care for the wounded, but far away from the fighting.

THE END

To follow another path, turn to page 9.
To learn more about the African front, turn to page 102.

The men in the ward aren't badly injured, but they still need care. You give them water and pain medicine. You examine wounds and change bandages. Some feverish men need cool cloths on their foreheads.

But mostly the soldiers need kindness. You smile and ask their names and where they're from. You hold their hands if they're frightened. Some tell you about their families or friends. A few want to talk about the battles they've seen. Others just stare into space, quietly. When your shift is over, you go to your own cot and collapse, exhausted.

The next day is quiet in the hospital. There are rumors that the battle is over. You hope they're true.

Turn the page.

The day after that is your day off. It's a relief to go with a group of nurses to explore a nearby village. You all have lunch at a small café. The war feels very far away. But then you hear the rumble of missile fire in the distance. A squadron of airplanes roars past.

Suddenly, an air-raid siren screeches overhead. An attack is coming! Some of the nurses don't think it's safe to travel until the attack is over. Others want to rush back to the hospital.

- To stay in the village, go to page 23.
- To return to the hospital, turn to page 26.

The café owner waves you to her cellar, and you all crowd inside. The ground trembles as bombs explode. Jars rattle on the shelves and dust shakes onto your heads. Eventually, the all-clear siren sounds. Slowly, you climb out of the cellar.

The café is a mess. Broken dishes and spilled food litter the floors. Outside, most of the town has been reduced to rubble. Several blood-covered people stumble through the streets in a daze. You take care of their injuries as best you can before you jump in the truck and race back to the hospital.

The road is lined with blackened craters and steaming, twisted metal from bombed trucks. When you get back, everything is chaos. Part of the roof collapsed into the recovery areas, killing several patients. People are frantically digging through the rubble for survivors.

Turn the page.

A U.S. soldier treats his fellow soldier's shrapnel wound.

When you hear the roar of truck engines outside, you realize with a sinking feeling that injured soldiers from the front are arriving. You step over the dead soldiers' bodies lining the hallway as the first wounded troops are lifted out of the trucks. There are too many injuries, too much to handle.

You go into shock. Hours later, your friends find you sitting on a sand dune, staring into the desert. A few days later, you're transported back to the United States and to a mental hospital. Your war experience is over, but it replays in your mind forever.

THE END

To follow another path, turn to page 9.
To learn more about the African front, turn to page 102.

You hang on to the side of the truck as it careens down the rough desert road. German and Italian fighter planes race toward the hospital. Would the enemy dare bomb a hospital? When you arrive, everyone is panicking. You help move patients to the lower levels. Those who can't walk are carried to safety. A bomb blast shakes the walls. Plaster and dust fill the air.

One of the doctors appears, saying the enemy is attacking your tanks a few miles away. There will be injured soldiers coming any minute. You should be ready for the wounded men. Some nurses and doctors rush to the main entrance, eager to bring in patients. But it might be safer to wait in the lower level.

- To go to the main entrance, go to page 27.
- To stay in the lower level, turn to page 28.

A crowd of nurses, doctors, and soldiers wait in the entryway. Far in the distance, you see tanks shooting at enemy planes flying overhead. One plane drops a bomb, and several tanks explode.

Suddenly, a screech fills the air. Before anyone can move, a bomb explodes near the hospital. Pain rips through your side. The last thing you remember is the smell of burning flesh before you pass out.

When you wake up, you're lying on a cot. It hurts to breathe. One of your fellow nurses takes your hand. She explains that a piece of shrapnel tore through your side. Several of your organs were damaged. You're going to a general hospital for surgery. From there, you'll probably be sent home. Your part in the war is over.

THE END

To follow another path, turn to page 9.
To learn more about the African front, turn to page 102.

You stay with the wounded soldiers in the lower level. Soon, an enormous explosion rocks the hospital. Equipment shatters. Chunks of wall crumble. A section of the roof collapses! You rush around, making sure the patients are all right. Several nurses and soldiers appear in the ward, covered in blood. You and the others claw at the rubble, trying to dig out any survivors. Your hands are raw and bloody from digging, but several patients are pulled out alive.

Finally, the roar of the planes disappears. The bombs stop. Ambulances begin to arrive. An officer tells you that the Allies won the battle. They have driven the Germans back for now. The bomb that hit the hospital was likely a stray bomb, he said, not a deliberate attack. Somehow, that makes you feel worse. So many died for a mistake.

The next day, word comes that the army is moving. The hospital is going with it. You welcome the distraction as you start preparing the wounded for transport. No one has any idea where you're headed or how long you'll be there. But you'll go wherever the soldiers need your help.

THE END

To follow another path, turn to page 9.
To learn more about the African front, turn to page 102.

Mobile field hospitals are set up about five or six miles from the front lines. When wounded soldiers arrive, doctors and nurses perform emergency surgeries on the worst cases. Most patients are sent on to the evacuation hospital. Soldiers with mild injuries are sent back to their units.

Wounded soldiers are given first aid on the front lines.

You spend the next hours assisting surgeons as they stitch wounds, perform surgeries, care for burns, and set broken bones. Some men can't be saved. Others are dead on arrival. You thought you were prepared for this work. But you've never seen such horrors.

That evening, word comes that medics at the front need emergency first-aid supplies. You volunteer to take the supplies.

Soon, you're driving a large truck packed with crates. It's pitch black in the desert at night. There are no lights anywhere except for the dust-covered ones on your truck. And the map you have is useless. None of the mobile unites are marked on it. When you get to a fork in the road, you don't know whether to turn right or left.

- To go right, turn to page 32.
- To go left, turn to page 36.

You turn right and drive for miles through the empty, dark desert. Finally, you reach a line of supply trucks following the troops. Soon, you'll be at the front.

An hour later, you hear the *pop-pop-pop* of gunfire. Someone yells, "Attack!" Shots light up the darkness. An explosion throws you out of the truck. You slam into the ground. It's dark, and you're surrounded by the chaos of battle. A soldier appears out of the darkness.

"Can you drive that?" he asks, pointing at your supply truck. You nod.

"Get to the clearing station and tell the commanding officer to send reinforcements." Then he disappears into the darkness.

Your heart thumps as you climb back into the truck. You see several wounded soldiers sitting alongside the road. They don't look seriously injured, but they do need medical attention. You have room in the truck for them.

- To help the soldiers into the truck, turn to page 34.
- To hurry on to the clearing station, turn to page 35.

Getting the injured men onto the truck takes longer than you thought. Finally, they're all inside. You arrive at the clearing station in about 10 minutes. It's a first-aid station at the front. Several medics rush to the truck to help the injured soldiers. One of the medics steps up to you.

"You've been shot," he says. "You're coming with me."

For the first time, you notice blood all over your uniform. Shocked, you faint, slumping against the medic. You wake up at the evacuation hospital the next day. The doctor tells you that you were shot twice. "You're lucky to be alive," he says. "And you saved three men as well."

THE END

To follow another path, turn to page 9.
To learn more about the African front, turn to page 102.

You rev the engine and race down the road, dodging troops and tanks. Missile fire lights up the sky. Tank blasts shake the ground. If you can make it past the fighting, it should be easy to get to the clearing station and deliver the message.

Suddenly, an explosion roars in your ears! The truck flies through the air. For a moment, it feels like you're floating. The truck lands, twisting into a heap of metal, with what's left of you inside. Someone else will have to deliver the message to the clearing station.

THE END

To follow another path, turn to page 9.
To learn more about the African front, turn to page 102.

Turning left was the right choice. A few miles ahead, you reach the clearing station. You slam on the brakes as four medics rush in front of the truck, carrying a stretcher. They're heading to the battle to look for wounded men.

You pull in as fighter planes roar overhead. You find a surgeon and tell him about the supplies. Then you pitch in to help. You give men water. You clean and bandage wounds.

By dawn, the battle is over. The surgeon tells you that the clearing station will be moved with the battalion. The most seriously injured will stay here with a unit of troops until they are well enough to be moved. He asks if you can stay for a day or two to help. You know that the hospital is expecting you back.

- To stay with the wounded, go to page 37.
- To return to the hospital, turn to page 38.

It feels strange being left behind, as the clearing station is packed up and loaded onto trucks. All that's left are a few small tents surrounded by miles of desert. The next day, several ambulances arrive. They take everyone to the evacuation hospital.

As the ambulances begin the long trip back, you see the destruction of battle. Piles of damaged and destroyed vehicles line the narrow road. Bomb craters dot the desert. You see a few downed airplanes. Some are still on fire. You can only imagine how awful the battle had been. From now on, you'll stay with the evacuation hospital.

THE END

To follow another path, turn to page 9.
To learn more about the African front, turn to page 102.

There are enough medics here to care for all the injured, so you return to the hospital. As the ambulance bumps along the desert road, you hear a plane overhead. A single German fighter plane flies into view. It looks like it's in trouble. It wobbles in the air and crashes to the ground.

A plume of smoke rises in the distance. It's likely the pilot died in the crash. But what if he survived and needs help? Is it worth the risk to help the enemy pilot?

- To see if the pilot is alive, go to page 39.
- To continue on to the hospital, turn to page 41.

You don't care if the pilot is a German.
It's your job to help people.

To your surprise, the pilot is alive, but barely.
Quickly, you bandage his bleeding wounds and
get him into the ambulance. The doctors are
surprised when you arrive with a German pilot.
You and another nurse prep him for surgery.

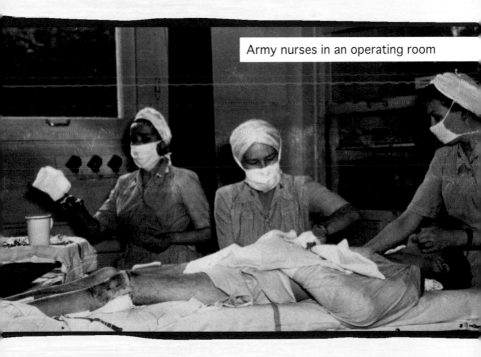

Army nurses in an operating room

Turn the page.

The pilot survives the surgery. A few days later, he is loaded into an ambulance and taken to another hospital to recover. After that, the British will send him to a Canadian prisoner of war camp. You watch the ambulance leave knowing you did the right thing. You saved a man's life, and there's one less enemy soldier to fight.

THE END

To follow another path, turn to page 9.
To learn more about the African front, turn to page 102.

You don't think anyone could have survived that crash. It's better that you focus on helping your own men. When you get back to the hospital, you see several German and Italian soldiers in the wards. They were captured by the Allied forces and brought here to treat their wounds. You put them into a small room away from the rest of the patients. They're all young and scared, just like the American soldiers. You show them kindness as they recover from their surgeries.

A few days later, they are sent to prisoner of war camps in Great Britain and Canada. You're glad you helped, but you're not sorry to see them go. Their cots will soon be filled with wounded and dying Allied soldiers, and you have a job to do.

THE END

To follow another path, turn to page 9.
To learn more about the African front, turn to page 102.

CHAPTER 3

NORTH AFRICAN WAR IN THE AIR

You grew up in the British countryside. As a teenager, you heard about German leader Adolf Hitler. He wanted to conquer all of Europe. On September 1, 1939, Germany invaded Poland. Poland and Great Britain are allies, so Great Britain declared war on Germany.

Soon, other countries joined the war. Japan and Italy joined Germany. They are known as the Axis countries. Great Britain and France joined Poland. They are the Allied forces. You're 20 years old, and World War II has begun.

Britain needs thousands of fighter pilots. You sign up for the Royal Air Force (RAF). At training camp, you take classes in math and engineering. You memorize different types of planes. You spend hundreds of hours learning how to fly. Doctors give you eye tests and physical exams. After six months, you're ready to go to war.

You're on your way to North Africa. There, British forces are fighting Italian and German armies. Pilots are needed to defend the island of Malta. It is an important supply port. There's also a need for photo reconnaissance pilots. These pilots spy on the enemy and take photos of troops and supplies.

- To defend Malta, turn to page 44.
- To do photo reconnaissance, turn to page 57.

Malta is a British colony on a small island in the Mediterranean. Before the war, it was a quiet place with beautiful towns. When World War II started, Malta's location made it an important resupply stop for Allied ships in North Africa. Hitler wants to control Malta. He ordered German planes to bomb the island. Now towns in Malta have been destroyed. The people are going hungry.

A heavily bombed street in Valletta, Malta

The Allies are sending a group of fighter pilots to defend Malta against the German Air Force. But Malta is too far out into the ocean for your Spitfire fighter planes to get to. So an Allied aircraft carrier is taking the planes to Malta. When the ship gets close, you and the other pilots will fly to the island. Your Spitfires have extra gas tanks so they can fly farther.

After days at sea, it's finally time to take off and fly to Malta. You can leave with the first group of pilots or wait for the second group.

- To leave with the first group, turn to page 46.
- To wait for the second group, turn to page 50.

It's smooth flying all the way to Malta.
You and the rest of the squadron land on the
airfield and gather in the mess hall. All that
flying made you hungry.

Suddenly, air-raid sirens go off. You're being
attacked! You and the other pilots rush out and
see a squadron of German planes flying low.
They drop bombs everywhere.

You need to get to a plane so you can defend
against this surprise attack. The planes in the
large, roofed hangar were protected from the
attack, so they weren't damaged by the bombs.
But they were also in the hangar for repairs.
The planes on the runway have taken some hits,
but they're closer. Maybe some can still fly.

- To fly a plane from the hangar, go to page 47.
- To fly a plane on the runway, turn to page 49.

You'd rather take your chance with a plane that hasn't been hit. You run to the hangar and jump in the nearest one. You start the engine. It seems to be working fine, so you take off. Only two other Spitfires are in the air along with you. Three against a dozen German planes isn't great. But you're here to defend Malta. That's what you're going to do.

An enemy plane opens fire but misses you. You fire. Nothing happens! The ammunition must have been taken out of the plane when it went in for repairs! With no bullets, the only thing you can do is lure them away from the airfield. You swoop in front of the German plane, hoping it will chase you. Sure enough, it turns and aims. You dodge, then dive, flying away from the airfield. The German plane keeps firing. Your Spitfire lurches to one side, its wing damaged.

Turn the page.

Frantically, you crash-land miles away from the airfield. German planes roar past and disappear. A column of black smoke rises from the airfield far away. The Germans won this round, you think grimly. Most of the Allied planes were damaged or destroyed in the attack. You limp out of the wreckage and wait for help to arrive. Even if you lose your leg, you're thankful to be alive.

THE END

To follow another path, turn to page 9.
To learn more about the African front, turn to page 102.

You make it to a plane that hasn't been hit. Quickly, you gun the engine and take flight on a thin strip of remaining airfield. Only a few pilots make it into the air. You're badly outnumbered, but you'll do what you can. The German planes fly over the airfield again and again, dropping bombs.

One enemy plane comes after you. It fires and misses. You return fire, sending the German plane to the ground. Another gives chase and then another. You shoot until you run out of ammunition. Then you see fire coming from your engine. The plane sputters, then takes a nosedive to the ground. Your time is up.

THE END

To follow another path, turn to page 9.
To learn more about the African front, turn to page 102.

The sky is blue and clear. You're glad to finally be in the air. From what you've heard about Malta, the people desperately need your help.

Halfway to the island, you see puffs of smoke coming from your engine. You don't know what's wrong, but you need to land as soon as possible.

Finally, you see the island stretched out below you. Then far in the distance, you see several black specks. You hear the rumble of plane engines. It's a group of German planes!

Your heart pounds as you grip the plane's joystick. There's a gray button on it. Pressing it fires weapons at the enemy. You hope you don't have to use it.

The other Spitfire pilots are zooming toward the enemy, guns firing. Smoke is pouring from your engine. Your plane can't take much more. You can do a tricky spin to dodge the gunfire. Or you can gun the engine for speed and try to outrun them.

- To dodge their gunfire, turn to page 52.

- To pile on the speed and try to lose the German planes, turn to page 55.

A German bomber dives toward you. You spin your wings, dodging the machine-gun fire. Flames burst from your engine. You only have a few seconds to decide what to do next. You can return fire and try to safely crash-land. Or you can eject and parachute to the ground.

- To try to crash-land safely, go to page 53.
- To parachute to safety, turn to page 54.

You press the gray button and hope you're aiming in the right direction. A roar of gunfire heads toward the German fighter plane. Smoke billows from beneath the plane. It nosedives to the ground. You don't see it crash. You're trying to land your own plane.

You spot a large farm field close by. You drop the landing gear and hit the green field, sliding to a jarring stop. In a panic, you jump out of the plane and run. The engine explodes, sending a fireball across the field. You're relieved to be alive as you start the long walk to the airfield. When you get there, you'll find out how many of your fellow pilots survived.

THE END

To follow another path, turn to page 9.
To learn more about the African front, turn to page 102.

You have to ditch the plane. You pop open the cockpit cover and jump, then pull your parachute cord. Your plane plunges to the ground and crashes in a fiery heap below. You're glad you weren't in it.

Suddenly, your parachute twists in the wind. One of the German planes has shot through your parachute. You grip the cords as you fall faster, the parachute flapping uselessly above you. You close your eyes and feel the wind on your face for the last time.

THE END

To follow another path, turn to page 9.
To learn more about the African front, turn to page 102.

You roar past the German plane at top speed. One of the other Spitfire pilots appears and opens fire. Before the German pilot knows what's happening, his plane is falling from the sky. The German pilot pulls his parachute and floats toward the ground. If he survives, he'll be taken as a prisoner of war.

British Spitfires

Turn the page.

Quickly, you and the other pilot land on the airfield. As you head to the hangar, several loud explosions get your attention. The Germans are bombing the airfield! You run for your life as the German planes attack.

Afterward, they rise into the sky and disappear. Every Allied plane has been destroyed. It's a blow to the Allied forces on Malta. It will be weeks before the field is rebuilt and more Spitfires arrive. You're just glad you survived the attack. Now you can help rebuild.

THE END

To follow another path, turn to page 9.
To learn more about the African front, turn to page 102.

You're assigned to a photo spy team in North Africa. These pilots are nicknamed "Photo Joes." They fly into enemy territory to photograph troops, weapons, aircraft, buildings, and weather. The photos are used to gather information on the enemy and plan attacks. Your Spitfire plane doesn't have any weapons. They've been removed to make the plane lightweight and fast. You're expected to fly high and dodge the enemy. Your plane is painted light blue and gray to blend in with the sky.

Each recon plane has five cameras to take hundreds of photos. To take photos, you press a button. After you complete a mission, you bring the film to a special photo lab back at the base. There, the film is developed into photos and studied.

Turn the page.

Crews rearm and refuel Spitfires in Malta.

You have two missions to choose from.
One is to fly over the North African coast to spy
on ships in the area. Another is to head to the
desert to report on enemy troop movements.

- To fly over the coast, go to page 59.
- To take the desert mission, turn to page 66.

Your information tells you that Italian ships are moving toward the North African coast. You fly high and fast, watching the ocean below.

Finally, you spot the ships. But they're not Italian—they're German. This is very important information.

Suddenly, a loud *BOOM* comes from one of the ships, then another. They're firing their antiaircraft guns at you! But your little Spitfire is fast enough to dodge them.

A stream of gunfire whizzes past. That was closer than you'd like. If you keep flying over, you risk getting hit. But if you fly back now, you won't get any photos.

- To finish the mission, turn to page 60.
- To retreat, turn to page 64.

The gunfire is only coming from two of the ships. You zoom over the ships, staying out of range of the guns. You click the cameras furiously, taking the pictures you need.

Without warning, the camera button on your joystick jams. You frantically press the button several times. Finally, it unsticks. But you've missed photographing some ships. With a sinking feeling, you realize you have to make a second run. You don't want to face those guns again. If you leave now, you might have enough photos.

- To make a second run, go to page 61.
- To return to base with the photos you have, turn to page 62.

You turn around for your second run. You take a deep breath and swoop down as fast as the Spitfire can go. Instantly, the two ships open fire.

You're going to get those photos! You zoom past the large, heavy guns. They can't turn fast enough to track you. You zip over the fleet, cameras clicking. You've got the photos! With a whoop, you pull up to get out of range.

The plane shudders. You've been hit! The Spitfire wobbles and sputters, but it holds together until the airbase comes into view below. You make a rough landing, but you and the plane are in one piece. Hopefully, the photos will help the commanders plan the next attack.

THE END

To follow another path, turn to page 9.
To learn more about the African front, turn to page 102.

You climb to the clouds, out of range of the guns. You return to base and hand the film over to the photo lab crew. In just a few hours, all the photos are ready. Your commander calls you into his office.

"Looks like the ships are German, not Italian?" he asks, surprised. You nod.

Royal Air Force Spitfire

"This is useful information," he replies. "But why didn't you complete your mission?" he asks.

"The camera button stuck," you reply, ashamed. "I was taking heavy fire, sir. I decided not to risk a second run."

The commander glares at you.

"Your orders were to get those photos," he said. "Now someone else has to risk their life to get them. You're grounded."

It's an embarrassing end to your flying career.

THE END

To follow another path, turn to page 9.
To learn more about the African front, turn to page 102.

You climb beyond the range of the guns and turn toward the coastline. Even though you were in great danger, you're sure you'll be grounded for not completing the mission. As you approach the shore, you see several Italian battleships. They aren't supposed to be there! Quickly, you swoop down, taking photos as you go. The Italians weren't expecting you. They don't have time to attack. You zoom away before they can fire a shot.

Back at base, you hand the film over and go to your commander.

"Sir, I didn't complete the mission I was assigned," you begin.

He glares at you but nods for you to continue.

"I encountered heavy antiaircraft fire, too thick to survive," you continue.

"On my way back to base, I stumbled upon the Italian fleet. I got photos of those ships instead."

You stand, head down. The commander stares at you.

"I should ground you for failing your mission," he says. "But you made a judgment call to save your life and your equipment. I respect that. I'm also impressed at your quick thinking to take photos of the fleet you found instead."

He pauses. "Don't fail another mission. Understood?"

You vow never to fail a mission again.

THE END

To follow another path, turn to page 9.
To learn more about the African front, turn to page 102.

Your mission is to spy on enemy troops and tanks far out in the desert. Every day for the next week, you take photos of them. You fly during the day when visibility is the best. At first, you're afraid you'll be attacked. But the enemy doesn't move. No German planes chase you. By the end of the week, you're bored. Was this mission a complete waste of time?

As you prepare for your final run, your commander sends for you. He says the Allies are preparing for battle. But there are reports of a bad rainstorm in the area. He has orders to send a recon pilot to report on weather conditions. If you want the weather mission, he'll send another pilot to complete your desert mission.

- To report on the weather, turn to page 68.
- To finish your desert mission, turn to page 71.

Royal Air Force pilots learning navigation

You take off in your Spitfire and head into the desert. Weather recon is important. Armies must know what kind of weather to expect. A surprise storm can mean the difference between winning or losing a battle.

Dark clouds loom in the distance. It's a huge desert thunderstorm. These storms can turn roads into impassible mud. You take photos above and around the storm. The plane shakes and jumps in the wind as you rise above the clouds. You circle several times, taking hundreds of photos. As you turn for home, you think you see a dark shadow on the desert floor. It could be an area of especially heavy rain. But it could also be enemy troops. To find out, you'd have to fly into the storm to get a closer look. And your commander wants these photos as soon as possible.

- To return to base, go to page 69.
- To see what the shadow is, turn to page 70.

You return to base and hand the film to a camera crew. While they develop it, you tell the weather officers about the storm. When the photos are ready, they're sent to experts at interpreting weather in the photos. They'll add the information on a huge battle map. This is the map the commanders use to plan an attack.

Later, you find out that the weather information you collected made the general decide to delay an attack. He calls you into his office and congratulates you on your flying skills. You're proud of your work on the recon mission.

THE END

To follow another path, turn to page 9.
To learn more about the African front, turn to page 102.

You take a deep breath and fly into the storm. Rain pelts the cockpit. Then the shadow becomes clearer. It's a large supply convoy of German trucks and tanks! You take dozens of photos. You hope the storm won't ruin the images.

A burst of wind slams you against the control panel. You hit your head hard. You're dizzy and bleeding, but you manage to regain control of the plane. By now, you're dangerously low to the ground, and there's no choice but to land.

You make a crash-landing. The plane is destroyed, but you manage to crawl out of the wreckage. Just then, German soldiers appear, pointing their guns. You spend the rest of the war in a prisoner of war camp.

THE END

To follow another path, turn to page 9.
To learn more about the African front, turn to page 102.

It's boring, but you'll see your mission through. One last time, you fly the familiar route. You look down in shock. The enemy is gone! You zoom low, taking photo after photo.

Suddenly, several German planes streak straight toward you! They don't want you taking pictures, that's for sure. A burst of gunfire tears off a piece of your Spitfire. You don't have any guns to defend yourself! Fortunately, speed and great flying can keep you alive. But maybe there's a way to force one of them to crash land.

- To try to outrun them, turn to page 73.
- To try to force one to crash-land, turn to page 74.

A Spitfire airplane

You pull up hard and fly high, racing as fast as the engine will go. Your Spitfire is lighter and faster than those German planes, so you stay ahead of them.

One breaks away from the rest and puts on a burst of speed. A hail of bullets tears away your tail. Before you can parachute out, another shower of gunfire hits the engine. It explodes into flames. The plane falls to the desert, bringing the photos, and you, to a fiery end.

THE END

To follow another path, turn to page 9.
To learn more about the African front, turn to page 102.

You soar into a bank of clouds and stay there until you think it's safe. Then you turn back. One German plane doesn't see you come out of the clouds. You emerge so close to its tail that you can almost touch it. Now's your chance. You gun your engine, forcing the enemy plane closer to the ground. The enemy loses control and crashes into the desert. You did it! Quickly, you race back to base.

A couple hours later, the commander asks for you.

"You got some great photos," the commander says. "But chasing that plane was foolish and dangerous. If you had crashed or been killed, we wouldn't know about those enemy planes. You're grounded."

He dismisses you without another word. To your shame, your photo recon career is over.

THE END

To follow another path, turn to page 9.
To learn more about the African front, turn to page 102.

CHAPTER 4

FIGHTING FOR THE DESERT AT SEA

On December 7, 1941, Japanese forces attacked Pearl Harbor, pulling the United States into World War II. Like most Americans, you were ready to defend your country. Within weeks, you volunteered for the U.S. Navy. After a six-week boot camp, you and thousands of other Navy recruits were sent to war at sea.

Turn the page.

The attack on Pearl Harbor

Life at sea is strict. Before dawn, a wake-up bell clangs. Everyone spills out of their hammocks and packs them away. Then it's time to clean the ship. Every sailor scrubs the deck until it's spotless. Then breakfast!

The rest of the day is spent cleaning and repairing machinery, doing drills, and practicing aiming and firing the guns. The ship must be ready for battle at any moment.

For weeks, your ship crisscrosses the ocean. It visits ports in Europe. No one knows what your mission is.

There are rumors that the ship is headed to North Africa. You've heard whispers of two secret Allied operations that your ship might be a part of.

Operation Pedestal is a mission to resupply the island of Malta. Malta is the perfect place to launch attacks on North Africa, Germany, and Italy. Both sides want to control Malta.

When the war began, the island was poorly defended. Italian and German bombers have attacked for weeks. A few Allied planes defended Malta.

Then the Germans made a blockade of ships around the island. No Allied supply ships could get through. The people of Malta were starving.

The Allies came up with a bold plan. They would build up a large group, or fleet, of ships to resupply Malta and defeat the enemy.

Turn the page.

The other mission is called Operation Torch. When the United States entered the war, the Allies began planning a huge attack in North Africa. Major General George Patton is the commander of the mission. If the Allies win, they will defeat Italy and Germany and control North Africa for good.

Major General George Patton

- To be a part of Operation Pedestal, go to page 79.
- To be a crew member on a ship in Operation Torch, turn to page 90.

You are on one of the ships that is part of this enormous fleet of ships. It is a very dangerous mission. The ocean near Malta is filled with enemy battleships, aircraft carriers, and submarines. Your fleet includes more than 50 battleships, destroyers, and aircraft carriers protecting the supply ships. You hope it's enough.

After several days, the fleet enters the Mediterranean. A German spy plane flies overhead. It's not long before enemy bombers fill the skies. Below the waves, enemy submarines head straight for you. Alarms scream from every part of the ship. It's time to get to your battle station!

- To take your station at the antiaircraft guns, turn to page 80.
- To defend against the submarines, turn to page 85.

Enemy bombers zoom in and drop bombs everywhere. Soon, several Allied ships are on fire. Allied fighter pilots chase the enemy planes all over the sky. You and the other gunners shoot at the enemy planes. Most of the time, your guns miss. Sometimes they don't, and an enemy plane falls into the ocean. Finally, late that evening, the German planes disappear, and the bombing stops. You catch a few hours of sleep. The attack starts again the next morning.

Axis fighter planes roar toward the fleet, dropping bombs. The Allied ships zigzag through the water, trying to avoid the submarines and mines. Later in the afternoon, more German planes appear. Your gun gets red-hot from all the shooting. Your ears are ringing from the roar of the guns.

Without warning, an explosion throws you to the deck. You don't know if your ship was hit by a mine or a torpedo. It doesn't matter, the ship is on fire! You know there must be injured crew members. You can assist the medics or help put out the fire.

- To help the injured crew, turn to page 82.
- To put out the fire, turn to page 84.

A German bomb exploded on the rear deck. Wounded men are lying everywhere. You help clean wounds and give first aid.

The battle rages all day and night. Axis forces hammer the Allied fleet. German submarines get through the defenses.

You watch Allied ships sink, one after another. The German planes and Italian submarines destroy all the Allied aircraft carriers.

The largest oil tanker, the *Ohio*, is hit many times but stays afloat. The Allied fleet is scattered, but the ships return fire, and dozens of enemy planes go down. The Allies suffer heavy losses, but several supply ships escape.

What's left of the supply fleet makes it to Malta the next afternoon. Even though many Allied ships and crew were lost, the mission to get supplies to Malta was a success. Amazingly, the *Ohio* is still afloat. Its cargo of oil will fuel the Allies' attacks for several months. You see the cheering crowds at the docks and know you're lucky to be on one of the few ships that survived.

THE END

To follow another path, turn to page 9.
To learn more about the African front, turn to page 102.

You grab a hose and join a group of sailors working frantically to put out the fire. The deck is slick with oil. You slip several times. The fire is bigger than you thought, and it takes some time to get it under control.

Suddenly, the oil catches fire. With a *whoosh*, flames race across the deck. Your oil-soaked uniform catches fire. Screaming, you drop to the deck and your crewmates put out the fire.

You're badly burned. They carry you to the sick bay. You're lucky to be alive, but your part in the battle is over.

THE END

To follow another path, turn to page 9.
To learn more about the African front, turn to page 102.

You are part of the crew in charge of dropping depth charges. Depth charges are underwater bombs. They are loaded on to a special machine on deck. The machine shoots them into the water. After a few seconds, the charges explode underwater. Depth charges destroy enemy submarines and keep them out of range of the ship.

The enemy planes and submarines keep coming. You see smoke billowing from an Allied aircraft carrier. It's been hit with torpedoes. It rolls on its side and sinks in eight minutes. Hundreds of survivors jump into the oil-covered water. The oil catches fire!

Turn the page.

A sailor watches as the HMS *Eagle* begins to sink.

You race out with a rescue crew and start pulling survivors out of the flaming water. One man is struggling to reach the lifeboat. You can jump into the water and help him. Or you can throw him a life jacket.

- To jump into the water, go to page 87.
- To throw him a life jacket, turn to page 88.

You're coughing from the smoke and oil smell, but you dive into the water. It's full of debris from the ship. Something bumps your head, but you're too focused on the rescue to notice. The man grabs your arm, almost pulling you under.

You get him to the boat. Several pairs of hands lift you both out of the oily water. As soon as the lifeboat is full, you take the survivors back to the ship. As you climb onto the deck, a wave of dizziness hits and you collapse.

You wake up in sick bay two days later! The doctor says you got a nasty head wound and never felt it. He also gives you the news that your ship, along with a few others, made it to Malta. Until you recover, you're out of the war.

THE END

To follow another path, turn to page 9.
To learn more about the African front, turn to page 102.

The man grabs the life jacket, and you pull him in. You tuck him into the boat and keep pulling others out of the water. When the boat is full, you take the survivors back to the ship. The lifeboat crews from your ship and others rescue more than 900 survivors.

The Axis forces continue to batter the Allied fleet. The sky fills with smoke, and the sound of planes roars overhead. Enemy bombers attack the fleet all evening, but none of your ships go down. You hear that one of the Allied battleships rammed and sank an Italian submarine!

The battle rages for the next two days. The enemy forces destroy more than half of the Allied fleet, including supply ships and aircraft carriers. One oil tanker, the *Ohio*, is badly damaged by torpedoes. It manages to barely stay afloat.

Finally, the remains of the fleet arrive in Malta. Hungry people line the docks, cheering and crying tears of joy at the sight of the ships. You're glad to have made it through.

THE END

To follow another path, turn to page 9.

To learn more about the African front, turn to page 102.

Your ship is headed for Fedala. It's a town on the coast of Morocco, a few miles north of Casablanca. That city is controlled by the Vichy French government. This group has split off from the main French government. It is fighting with Germany and Italy. Your ship is carrying thousands of Allied infantry soldiers. The secret plan is to unload the troops on land for a surprise attack on Casablanca. But Fedala and Casablanca are heavily guarded. You're sailing into danger.

It's the night before the attack, and you're on duty. The stormy weather tosses your huge ship like a bathtub toy. Your job is to help get the troops onto landing boats and to shore. But the boats have trouble in the storm. Many crash and sink. You panic as weapons, ammunition, and medical supplies are lost beneath the waves.

Finally, it's dawn. You hear the whine of planes above. The commander shouts, "The enemy has spotted us! Battle stations!"

The ship is taking fire from enemy bombers and from enemy ships at the docks. They are also shooting at the Allied troops on shore. You dash to your gun and jump into the seat. You can aim for enemy fighter planes above or the ships near shore.

- To fire at the planes, turn to page 92.
- To shoot at the ships, turn to page 99.

The air is filled with the roar of planes, explosions, and gunfire. You watch the planes battle one another overhead. They soar through the clouds, shooting, bursting into flames, and crashing into the sea. Enemy planes fly low and attack the Allied ships. American fighter pilots chase them. You manage to take out an enemy bomber.

One Allied plane flies low over the deck, its wing on fire. It lands in the water near the ship. The enemy plane that shot it down streaks by overhead. You can aim for it. Or you can try to rescue the pilot.

- To fire on the enemy plane, go to page 93.
- To try to rescue the pilot, turn to page 94.

The plane is moving fast, and you miss.

It zooms upward into the clouds, but not before it drops a final bomb onto the deck of the ship.

Amazingly, the bomb doesn't explode on impact.

Instead, it rolls toward your gun! Before you have time to leap to safety, the bomb explodes, blasting you and the gun into the ocean forever.

THE END

To follow another path, turn to page 9.
To learn more about the African front, turn to page 102.

You'd rather try to save a life than take one. You grab a life jacket and dive into the cold ocean. By now, the plane has gone under. The pilot is bobbing on the waves. You can't tell if he's still alive or not as you swim to him. Other crewmen drop a lifeboat. You climb into the small boat pulling the pilot with you. He's breathing, but he's totally knocked out. Once you're back on the ship, you carry the pilot to the sick bay. You hope he makes it.

As you leave the sick bay, the ship shudders. An explosion knocks you off your feet. The ship has been hit by a torpedo from a submarine! Luckily, the damage isn't enough to sink the ship. When you get back to your battle station, you see an enemy ship nearby. You can fire at it. But you really want to take out the submarine that hit you.

- To aim at the ship, go to page 95.
- To attack the submarine, turn to page 97.

You and your fellow gunners aim and shoot. The enemy ship returns fire. Your ship is hit a few times but isn't badly damaged. The enemy ship isn't so lucky. It explodes, sinking fast. For the rest of the afternoon, you stay at your station, shooting at enemy ships.

The next day, enemy forces surrender the city. The Battle of Casablanca is over.

Operation Torch is a success! But it came at a high cost. Hundreds of troops died trying to get ashore.

The Casablanca coast is littered with damaged Allied vessels. Bombed boats, trucks, and tanks cover the beaches. The huge enemy battleship is a pile of twisted metal.

Turn the page.

You catch a glimpse of General Patton as he passes by, standing tall on the deck of a small boat. You salute the commander who conquered Casablanca and helped the Allies to victory in North Africa. You're proud you were a part of it.

THE END

To follow another path, turn to page 9.
To learn more about the African front, turn to page 102.

Nearby, the crew launches depth charges into the ocean. These underwater bombs are designed to sink into the water, then explode. They can damage or destroy enemy submarines. Submarines will come to the surface to escape the deadly blast.

One by one, the depth charges explode underwater. You scan the waves, looking for enemy submarines. One appears! Quickly, you aim and fire. The submarine sinks back under the waves. You don't know if you hit it. Maybe the depth charge destroyed it. Or it might have fled the danger.

The battle rages on for another day. The Allied ships protect the invading troops by shooting at enemy ships. The fearless Allied bomber pilots protect you from above.

Turn the page.

Many Allied ships are destroyed and sunk, taking hundreds to the bottom of the sea. But the enemy has been hit hard too. Finally, the Axis forces surrender. Operation Torch is over. Now the Allies control Casablanca. Maybe it won't be long before you win all of North Africa.

THE END

To follow another path, turn to page 9.
To learn more about the African front, turn to page 102.

The enemy ships create smokescreens around themselves so they can't be seen. You can't tell where to shoot. Finally, a ship glides out of the smokescreen. Allied bombers zoom in and drop bombs. The ship bursts into flames and sinks. The battle rages through the day. The Allies take heavy losses, but you won't give up.

The next day, you see the enemy battleship, the *Jean Bart*, at the dock. But it's clearly damaged from yesterday's battle. It don't think it's still a threat. But as you approach the *Jean Bart*, it opens fire! The ship's crew secretly repaired it overnight. You can assist the Allied troops on land. Or you can fire on the *Jean Bart*.

- To help the troops on land, turn to page 100.
- To attack the *Jean Bart*, turn to page 101.

You start firing at a large gun battery on the beach. Several planes drop bombs. Soon, the enemy guns are destroyed. The Allies keep up the battle, firing on enemy ships. Fighter planes destroy several enemy submarines.

By the afternoon, it's clear that the Allies are winning. Later, officers announce that the enemy commander has surrendered. Operation Torch is a victory! It looks like the Allies might take control of North Africa after all.

THE END

To follow another path, turn to page 9.
To learn more about the African front, turn to page 102.

You fire at the *Jean Bart*'s large gun turret. Allied bombers drop bombs on the ship as well. A huge hole appears in the ship's side. Suddenly, an explosion rocks your ship. The blast knocks you unconscious.

You wake up in the sick bay. You've got a broken arm and a nasty lump on your head, but you'll recover. Another sailor tells you that the *Jean Bart* was destroyed in the fighting, and the battle is over. You're lucky to have survived this battle in the African campaign. So many others didn't.

THE END

To follow another path, turn to page 9.

To learn more about the African front, turn to page 102.

CHAPTER 5
VICTORY AT THE AFRICAN FRONT

By 1943, the war in Africa was over. It was one of the Allies' most important early successes. But victory came at a high cost. Thousands of Allied soldiers were killed or wounded on the desert battlefields.

The biggest threat to the Allied forces in North Africa was Nazi general Edwin Rommel, the Desert Fox. His Afrika Korps smashed through the British Army early in the campaign.

Another enemy the Allies faced in Africa was the pro-German French government known as Vichy France. They joined with Hitler and the Axis forces. Vichy France controlled parts of North Africa, including Morocco, Tunisia, and Algeria.

American forces joined the British in 1942. Operation Torch was the first battle that British and American forces fought together. The combined armies pushed the Axis forces out of Egypt. They reclaimed the area that Rommel had won. A few months later, the Axis forces surrendered.

The Allies had another, secret reason to fight in Africa. They wanted to distract Hitler from his battles in Europe. The Allies hoped Hitler would waste precious troops and supplies in Africa.

The plan worked, for a time. The fresh German troops won several desert battles against the Allies. But the Allied forces grew too strong. They destroyed many German and Italian supply ships. Rommel's armies became low on food, water, and equipment. This helped the Allies to finally win the African front.

The Allied hero of Operation Torch was General George Patton. Patton continued to lead the Allied forces until the end of the war.

Although the battles on the African front are not well known, they proved to be some of the most important events of the war. The Allied victory gave them control of North Africa, Malta, and the Suez Canal. The Allies used these vital areas to refuel and resupply troops in Europe. This paved the way for the Allies to win World War II.

MAP OF THE AFRICAN FRONT

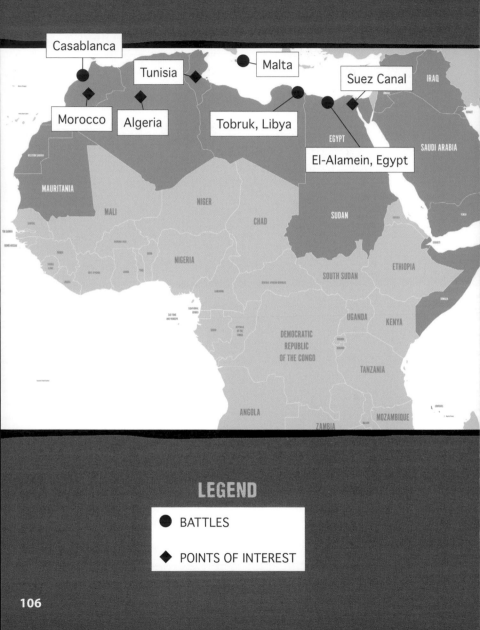

Casablanca

Tunisia

Malta

Suez Canal

Morocco

Algeria

Tobruk, Libya

El-Alamein, Egypt

LEGEND

● BATTLES

◆ POINTS OF INTEREST

TIMELINE

✦ **Sept. 1939**	Germany invades Poland. World War II begins.
✦ **Sept. 1940**	Italy invades Egypt.
✦ **Dec. 1941**	British forces defeat Rommel at Tobruk, Libya. Japan attacks Pearl Harbor, Hawaii. The United States enters the war.
✦ **Jan. 1942**	Rommel retakes Tobruk from the British forces.
✦ **July 1942**	Allies win the First Battle of El-Alamein against Rommel's forces.
✦ **Aug. 1942**	Operation Pedestal succeeds.
✦ **Oct. to Nov. 1942**	Allies win the Second Battle of El-Alamein and score victory with Operation Torch.
✦ **May 1943**	Axis troops surrender in North Africa.
✦ **May 7, 1945**	Germany surrenders, ending the war in Europe.
✦ **Aug. 1945**	U.S. drops atomic bombs on the Japanese cities of Hiroshima and Nagasaki. Japan surrenders.

OTHER PATHS TO EXPLORE

In this book, you've explored several key operations that took place in North Africa during World War II. But the experiences of those who went through these situations were just a part of what it was like to live and serve during World War II. How might your perspective change in a different situation?

1. During the war, Allied forces captured thousands of enemy prisoners of war (POWs). Many German and Italian POWs were shipped to camps in the United States. Imagine you live near one of these camps. The prisoners get good food and comfortable beds. Some of your loved ones were killed by German and Italian troops. Do you think it's fair that these men are allowed to live, while American soldiers risk their lives?

2. When World War II began, women weren't allowed in the military. But there weren't enough men to do all the war jobs. About 350,000 women served in military positions as nurses, pilots, mechanics, and more. At home, women worked in factories, building war supplies. When the war ended, many women wanted to keep their jobs. But they had to give them up to the men returning home. Imagine you're one of these women. How would this situation make you feel?

GLOSSARY

blockade (blok-AYD)—a closing off of an area to keep people or supplies from going in or out

colony (KAH-luh-nee)—a territory settled by people from another country and controlled by that country

evacuation (ih-vak-yoo-AY-shun)—the removal of large numbers of people leaving an area during a time of danger

invade (in-VAYD)—to send armed forces into another country in order to take it over

Mediterranean Sea (meh-dih-tare-AY-nee-uhn SEE)—a sea located between Europe, North Africa, and Western Asia

reconnaissance (ree-KAHN-uh-sents)—a mission to gather information about an enemy

shrapnel (SHRAP-nuhl)—pieces that have broken off from an explosive shell

Suez Canal (SOO-ez kuh-NAL)—a canal in northeast Egypt that connects the Mediterranean to the Red Sea

SELECT BIBLIOGRAPHY

Holocaust Encyclopedia
encyclopedia.ushmm.org/content/en/article/allied-military-operations-in-north-africa

Imperial War Museums
iwm.org.uk/history/second-world-war

National Army Museum
nam.ac.uk/explore/struggle-north-africa-1940-43

National Museum of the United States Air Force
nationalmuseum.af.mil/

National Museum of the U.S. Navy
history.navy.mil/content/history/museums/nmusn.html

The National World War II Museum
nationalww2museum.org/war/articles/us-invasion-north-africa

U.S. Army Center of Military History
history.army.mil/html/reference/army_flag/ww2_eame.html

READ MORE

Adams, Simon. DK Eyewitness. *World War II*. DK Children, 2021.

Mooney, Carla. *Historic Battles from World War II for Kids*. Emeryville, CA: Rockridge Press, 2021

Rasmussen, R. Kent. *World War II Q&A: 175+ Fascinating Facts for Kids*. Emeryville, CA: Rockridge Press, 2021

INTERNET SITES

Britannica Kids: World War II
kids.britannica.com/kids/article/World-War-II/353934

DK FindOut! World War II
dkfindout.com/us/history/world-war-ii/

National Geographic Kids: 10 Facts About World War II
natgeokids.com/uk/discover/history/general-history/world-war-two/

ABOUT THE AUTHOR

Allison Lassieur is an award-winning author of more
than 150 history and nonfiction books about everything
from Ancient Rome to the International Space Station.
Her books have received several *Kirkus* starred reviews
and Booklist recommendations, and her historical novel
Journey to a Promised Land was awarded the 2020 Kansas
Library Association Notable Book Award, and Library
of Congress Great Reads Book selection. Allison lives in
upstate New York with her husband, daughter, a scruffy,
lovable mutt named Jingle Jack, and more books than she
can ever read.